Fascination of
Fire
Charcoal

Many thanks to Dan Phillips, Kate Hookham, Steven White and Petra Babikova, for their contribution and in making this book possible.

Special thanks go to all the children for whom we are in contact with on a daily basis for their joy and inspiration.

The rights of Claire Warden to be identified as the author of this work have been asserted in accordance with the copyright Designs and Patents Act 1988

Design and layout by Almond www.almondtds.com +44 (0)131 553 5523

Printed by J. Thomson Colour Printers, Glasgow, UK

Photography by Claire Warden and the Kindergarten teams.

All photographs © Mindstretchers Ltd

ISBN 978-1-906116-11-8

If you would like training materials or further information about the Fascination series or any other Mindstretchers publication please contact:
enquiries@mindstretchers.co.uk

Mindstretchers™
Glenruthven Mill
Abbey Road
Auchterarder
PH3 1DP
Scotland, UK

T: +44 (0)1764 664409
F: +44 (0)1764 660728
E: enquiries@mindstretchers.co.uk
www.mindstretchers.co.uk

Foreword
by Tim Gill
Author of No Fear, Growing up in a risk averse society

A good friend who grew up in the Suffolk countryside told me that as a child, most summer holidays, he would rarely leave the house without his tin of 'punk': a heap of dried, decayed wood and leaves used for starting a campfire. As a Woodcraft Folk volunteer, I have seen the intense, determined expression on an eight-year-old child's face as she tries to light a ball of cotton wool with a fire steel. Her childhood is very different to my friend's. But they share an appetite for adventure and discovery.

Those of us who want to offer children engaging, adventurous, stimulating experiences face a profound challenge. As children ourselves, we explored the everyday wonders of the world under our own steam, and in our own way. The formative nature of these experiences was amplified by the fact that we were in control. The children we work with rarely enjoy this freedom.

In her book Claire Warden shows how we can overcome this challenge. With charcoal as an organising theme, it reveals and respects the experiments, trials, mistakes, and sustained investigations that can be carried out by the children. How do we make charcoal? How do we keep the embers glowing? What can we use to grind down the lumps? What can we do with ground charcoal anyway? (A girl mixes it with water to make ink for drawing, while a boy uses the same substance to paint his skin, readying himself for a game of hide-and-seek in the woods.) What kind of stick is best for writing with charcoal ink – and what kind of surface?

Fire is a destructive, potentially dangerous force of nature. Adults who use it in their work with children need to take a thoughtful, balanced approach: giving children freedom to explore, discover and make their own stories and meanings, while managing the situation, so that children are not at risk of serious harm. The benefit-risk assessments described here are the perfect tool for supporting such an approach.

Of course we need to make links with good educational practice, and those links are here in abundance. But we also have another duty: to compensate children for the everyday freedoms that they may have lost compared to previous generations. The true value of this little gem of a book is that it respects the power of allowing children to have their own adventures, follow their own imaginations and make their own discoveries.

Contents

Introduction

Children find fascinating moments in every day, things to be fascinated by or in. Csíkszentmihályi (1990), refers to a state of mind which is all encompassing called the point of flow. Children need time to 'be', to process and to consider the world around them, to allow an enquiring mind to follow its own fascinations so that it can reach a deeper connection. In an education system with a focus on curriculum, a group of researchers came together and started to consider a key question.

'How do we deliver a 'curriculum' through children's fascinations, so that it can be used globally as a methodology for teaching and learning irrespective of the age of the child?'

This series of books is the result of that enquiry. They follow the fascinations of children from three to eleven years old, that we have worked with in play based environments and also in more structured school environments over a number of years.

When we consulted adults, they highlighted a number of issues that were barriers to the promotion of outdoor learning. Skill, knowledge and enthusiasm of the adult; observation of learning; identification and implementation of progression steps; coverage of the curriculum concerns surrounding risk. These issues have structured the content of the books. We hope that an enthusiastic mood overtakes the reader when they read the children's voices, wherever they are in the world.

In order to frame the series, we have taken the natural elements as our guide, Fire, Earth, Air and Water. These give us elements that can then be divided into smaller, deeper fascinations such as charcoal, mud, clouds, a puddle. These simple, natural materials conceal the fact that they support complex learning that easily overtakes an inter curricula approach to teaching and learning.

C. Warden.

Claire Warden February 2012

Chapter 1. What is Charcoal?

How do we see charcoal?

Charcoal is a material that we often overlook; it's the black stuff that gets left behind after a fire; the stuff that smudges and gets on your clothes and makes the garden look messy. It can have further negative connotations as it is usually the evidence of a fire being had in the wrong place, for example, if a person decides to illegally have a fire at the bottom of a tree, we will see the evidence through the charcoal remains at the tree trunk. Just as we perhaps are having fires less and less in recent times due to central heating systems, gas fires and other ways in which we keep warm, we are also becoming distant from resources such as charcoal. The word 'resource' is used purposefully because that is what charcoal is, a resource which has a myriad of different uses. When we think of charcoal today, the first image we may think of will be the bag of charcoal that we buy from the supermarket for cooking our barbeque, but its uses have been and continue to be rather more complex than this.

What is it?

Wood is made of carbon and volatile elements such as cellulose and water. When wood is put on a fire, the cellulose and water are the ingredients that will evaporate off first, leaving mainly the carbon components behind (which give the wood its strong black colour). When we carry on burning the black wood it will eventually turn to an ember, burning red hot until we are left only with ash. When we make charcoal, we burn off the cellulose and water just like in a normal fire but control the heat of the fire so that the black wood does not turn to embers and burn away, as this black stuff is the charcoal we want to keep. We control the heating of the wood by limiting the amount of oxygen that gets to it.

Charcoal can be made from all types of wood and this is generally the most common type of charcoal that we use. Lots of people also recommend using coconut skins for making charcoal. We can, however, create charcoal from different polymer cloths, or from animal remains and the reason for this is that they both have carbon in them. We as humans have carbon in us, so essentially one could make charcoal from a human body.

The structure of Charcoal

The carbon atoms in charcoal are structured intricately in a complex web and if we were to look at them through a microscope, we would not be able to make out a pattern. This is different from other carbon materials such as graphite, which is typically used in our pencils. The carbon in graphite is structured in fixed layers which is why it can be scraped off very easily. The complex and disorganised makeup of the carbon atoms in charcoal creates a very large surface area, which is the major reason why charcoal is used in many circumstances as a purifier, as the large surface area encourages infectious particles to stick to it.

How is it made?

The reason why you are able to make charcoal from wood, instead of it just burning away like a normal fire is because the oxygen element is taken away. We may make charcoal as a by product of a normal fire if we put too much wood over the top of a fire and so suffocate the wood below, or when we put a fire out with water when there is wood still not burnt away. However, when people want to intentionally make charcoal they will make a kiln. A kiln is basically something that we make to keep heat in – a bit like an oven. What people have done throughout history when trying to make charcoal, is to pile up lots of wood, cover the top of it with mud, clay, moss, so that oxygen cannot readily get in, and then light the wood from beneath (ensuring there is at least a hole where some air can get out). These people will also create little inlets in the outside of the kiln, so that they can let in more oxygen if they need. If the fire within the kiln is managed appropriately, then the wood will continue to heat but in a controlled manner, so that it does not get too hot that the wood starts to burn.

This is perhaps best summed up by a wonderful scene from Arthur Ransome's Swallows and Amazon's:

'We want ours to burn good and slow,' said Young Billy. 'If he burns fast he leaves nowt but ash. The slower the fire the better the charcoal.'

Susan was watching carefully.

'Why doesn't it go out?' she asked.

'Got too good a hold,' said Young Billy. 'Once he's got a good hold you can cover a fire up and the better you cover him the hotter he is and the slower he burns. But if you let him have plenty of air there's no holding him.'

Arthur Ransome, 'Swallows & Amazons,' 1930.

What is it used for?

Fuel

Charcoal has been traditionally used as a fuel for a variety of purposes. It was the fuel used by blacksmiths in the forges and it was used again as the main fuel for people working with metals such as iron. It was also used widely for the smelting process, whereby metal workers worked with metal to make new ones. The classic image that we have of a blacksmith banging a piece of iron over red hot embers is most likely to be charcoal. And the question to why charcoal was preferred by blacksmiths and other workers, can be answered plainly with the fact that charcoal has to get exceedingly hot before it burns away, meaning that a charcoal fire will be hotter and last longer – perfect then for working with metal. We can perhaps relate to this a little if anyone has ever used charcoal on a barbeque. Generally, when using this fuel you have to light it (which often seems to take a long time and then when it is lit, it pretty much just starts smoking – leaving you to think that it's going to go out). Then, leave it for a good hour or so until you come back to it (if you have done it correctly), the charcoal pieces have turned a white colour and in amongst them there is a burning red hot glow. If you have ever lit a fire, either outside, or in your living room, if you have managed to light it the wood generally starts burning straight away and you can see yellow flames, but of course it's not long before you have to keep adding more wood to keep the fire hot. Through this basic example, you can see that the use of charcoal is much more efficient and why so many workers throughout history have tried so hard to make it on a large scale. Even today, environmentalists and sustainable energy experts are putting forward ideas for creating charcoal from green plants and organic waste that will provide efficient energy.

In fact, for a period of time, charcoal was perhaps our most widely used fuel for both domestic and industrial purposes, and is perhaps the main reason why so much deforestation occurred in Britain. This is also the reason why woodland management techniques, such as coppicing were used so widely. Coppicing is implemented by cutting back the branches of trees to encourage more shoots to grow from one trunk, meaning that there will be a lot more smaller trunks of wood to work with. If you walk through certain woodlands in the UK, you can identify these coppiced areas when there maybe up to ten trunks coming from one spot, where normally you might expect just one tree to be. The use of charcoal as a fuel, was reduced significantly when fears surrounding the large amount of deforestation in the UK led to the introduction of coal. When coal took over as this main fuel, the use of charcoal was reduced dramatically – which is perhaps why we may only know about charcoal when we have barbeques!

In the arts

Charcoal is used widely in poetry due to its quite unique attributes. Its ubiquitous blackness and its associations with permanent change and death, make it a fascinating object to be used in all sorts of creative writing by poets, such as Emily Dickinson. The way that it can be touched, smelt, listened to and even tasted, adds to its creative literary appeal.

'Whirling Wind'

'Tree'

'Frog and Pond'

'Stuff'   'Smokey Fire'

Charcoal as a drawing material provides opportunity to experiment with shading, rubbings and texture, and supports an expressive style of art. It has been used widely as a tool for making art in cave paintings, such as the example in Lascaux Roufignac in France and particularly in pieces by Picasso and Dürer. And contemporary artists, such as David Nash have made use of charcoal as a medium for creating art.

As a purifier

Due to the structural form of carbon within charcoal, it is used effectively as a purifier. Many domestic water filtering systems use charcoal, and if camping out in the wild, a simple homemade charcoal water filter can provide a camper with clean drinking water (see adult skills section). Charcoal was also used in gas masks in World War One to filter the air from chemical bombs. Charcoal's properties for purifying has led to its use in medicines. People may take charcoal biscuits as a dietary supplement to help with gastric problems. Charcoal is also thought to have anti-oxidant properties and is also used by some to help preserve the goodness in food, for example, in cooked rice as it can absorb the impurities in cooking water and will help stop the growth of mould.

Chapter 2. Case Studies with Analysis and Possible Lines of Development

Case Study 1 – Transforming wood into charcoal

1. Exploring leftover charcoal from a fire

(i) Charcoal is often left behind in the fire pit as a discarded item. It is a bi-product of creating fire that offers children the chance to explore creative mark making, and the transformative effects of fire.

(ii) Often in the outdoor area, Nature provides an unexpected moment which is full of possibilities. These case studies begin to reveal the learning within such encounters.

During an afternoon out in the garden, several children explored the left over pieces of charcoal. One of the 3 year old boys collected all the loose bits of charcoal in a metal bucket and then picked the big ones to write his name on a rock. While he was beginning to write he exclaimed, "I've got two stones on the fire. I'm making a name."

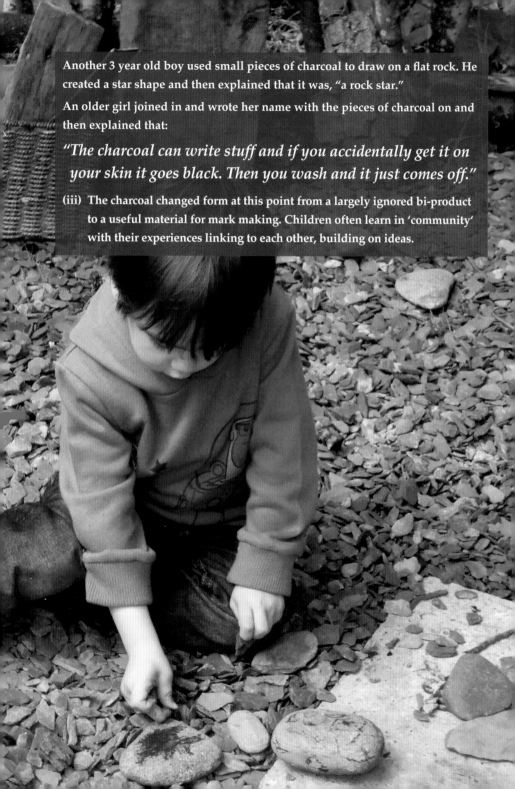

Another 3 year old boy used small pieces of charcoal to draw on a flat rock. He created a star shape and then explained that it was, "a rock star."

An older girl joined in and wrote her name with the pieces of charcoal on and then explained that:

"The charcoal can write stuff and if you accidentally get it on your skin it goes black. Then you wash and it just comes off."

(iii) The charcoal changed form at this point from a largely ignored bi-product to a useful material for mark making. Children often learn in 'community' with their experiences linking to each other, building on ideas.

2. Making a charcoal stick

During a session around the fire, several children started burning the end of a wooden stick in the fire (please see introduction and risk assessment for working with children around a fire). Due to the small ratios that we had for that day, it was decided to explore this further. In particular, a young boy and two young girls started to heat up the end of their sticks.

When the sticks were hot enough, the children removed the sticks and watched as the smoke disappeared into the air. One of the girls described that. "I took my stick out of the fire and held it out and all the smoke came out from the end. I thought WOW! We were also waving our sticks around to make some pictures in the air and then we started blowing them to make more smoke."

One of the young girls then noticed that when she blew on it the stick began to glow, exclaiming:

"It's like magic, the smoke stopped and I started blowing it to make an orangie, redie thingie at the end. Just awesome, awesome."

After exploring the sticks, the young boy started to rub the end of his smoke stick on a rock until the ash had fallen off, leaving only the blackened wood. He then used a different rock and began to write with the end of his stick.

After observing the boy write his name with his stick, the girls decided that it would be better to put water over the end of the stick to, "Make the smoke stop and to make a charcoal stick, so that we could draw on the stones." They then proceeded to soak the end of their sticks underneath the running water until they were happy they were 'ready'.

The girls then both began to use their sticks for drawing with on stones and for writing on pieces of log. When asked about the experience, one of the girls described, "Well, I didn't do pictures, I did writing on it, an E for Emily and then I did one for myself too." They dipped their sticks into a large chunk of charcoal when they needed more of the writing to be darker, and then spent time creating their designs on the flat pieces of rock.

3. Making an ember bowl

The children collected dry sticks from the woodland floor and sorted them into different piles according to size. One of the older boys wanted to create some wood shavings with his own penknife, so he carefully cut wood shavings and added them to the wood pile. The children then arranged the wood into a tipi like structure, taking time to carefully balance the different size sticks against each other. When they were happy with the structure, they added pieces of cotton wool that had been dipped into Vaseline. Jameel, an 8 year old boy , told the staff members that, "We use Vaseline because it helps the cotton wool burn."

The children used a flint made of magnesium to try to light the fire. When used correctly, the flint creates a spark that will set the cotton wool alight. They each had three turns at trying to create a spark with the flint and then passed it on to the next person. Once they had practiced making a spark, they passed the flint around again, but this time attempting to light the fire itself. One of the girls described that, "We use a whittler . . . er, I mean flint because it helps start the fire." (Anna aged 8 years).

Once the cotton wool had been lit, the children watched as each of the small dry sticks started to warm up, so much that they began to burn. The eldest girl and one of the boys then started to blow on the fire and the others watched as the flames started to rise higher. The boy blowing on the fire, described to the staff how, "We blow on the fire because it helps the fire get oxygen."

Anna held the ember in place using a stick. She tried several times before she was comfortable blowing on the ember and balancing the stick on it at the same time. She described that, "The trick is to blow hard enough, so that the ember starts to burn, but not too hard or you'll blow it out." When asking about her experience blowing the ember into the wood, she described that, "It's like keeping the sun alive. The sun is a big giant ember. It's like you are looking after the sun's child."

Each of the children were fixated with their embers as it gradually started to heat up the wood around it. The more each of them blew on their ember, the hotter they found the wood was getting. "It's burning the wood, look!"exclaimed one of the boys as he continued to watch the wood start to burn.

Once she had continued to blow on the ember, the hotter the wood around it became and noted as the wood became so hot, that she could simply blow straight on the wood and it would start to burn itself. Once the burning was complete, she used a piece of sandpaper to scrape away all of the burnt wood. One of the boys explained that, "You sand it down in the middle, so you don't get all the dust on it."

She then used a carving knife to whittle the outside bark from the wood until the whole bowl was smooth. To finish the bowl, she used the sandpaper to smooth over the wood. The children discussed what they could do with their bowls and it was suggested that they be used as candle holders.

Analysis of Learning – Case Study One

1. Exploring leftover charcoal from a fire

In each of the learning experiences here, the children are experimenting with charcoal as a material and have discovered its use for drawing, mark making and writing. The variety of pictures which highlight the way that the charcoal is used differently by all of the children, shows the high level of creativity that this type of discovery learning can support. When the three year old boy talks about 'stones on a fire,' we can infer that he has made the link between the fire and where charcoal comes from, which can be used as an effective starting point for exploring the effect of heat on wood.

PLODS

1) Explore charcoal as a tool for creating art. Look at different artistic techniques such as rubbings, shading, line and use of texture to support creative expression. Provide examples of famous pieces by Picasso and Dürer.

2) Experiment with charcoal as a material and look at ways we can manipulate it by grinding, breaking or mixing, and decide on different ways we can use it in the school environment.

3) Investigate how charcoal is made by discussing the effect of temperature in a real fire, focusing on the way the wood changes under heat.

2. Making a charcoal stick
3. Making an ember bowl

When we analyse the learning in these two scenarios, it is of no surprise that we should start by talking about risk and personal safety. The children here are given the freedom to interact with the fire and so the degree of personal responsibility is high. The concentration and decision making required in order to manage the risk in this environment, provides a range of rich learning for the children involved. The close interaction that the children have with the fire allows them to experience the fire through all of their senses from the smell of the smoke, crack of the flames to the glowing ember on the stick. These sensorial experiences provide a rich learning experience that will increase their knowledge about fire, wood, their own personal safety and well being. Being able to watch as the dry yellow wood changes in their hands to a glowing ember and then finally to charcoal, is an opportunity for them to see a chemical reaction occur before their eyes, a rich experience that can serve as the perfect platform to talk about the components of carbon and water in wood and the reason for the wood turning black – this conceptual knowledge can begin to be discussed with children from the age of three. Both the charcoal stick and ember bowl making process, allow the children to experience the effect of oxygen on a fire. The ember bowl making in particular, requires the children to give the ember a constant supply of oxygen and the more they blow on it, the warmer it gets, adding to their conceptual knowledge about what a fire needs to burn.

The sanding of the ember bowl in order to get rid of the charred wood, allows the children to learn about charcoal as a material, and to see that the chemical reaction taking place as a result of the transfer of heat, only occurs at the top of the wood.

In both of these scenarios, we see a lot of perseverance and patience as the ember bowl in particular, takes a very long time to get hot and to start burning down quickly. This, of course, is a positive learning outcome in itself and when we step back and analyse the level of engagement shown by the children involved, we can see further learning benefits of this. The experiences encourage a sense of control in the children, as they have to find a level of balance when managing the ember in their piece of wood, which is best summed up when the young girl says, "The trick is to blow hard enough so that the ember starts to burn but not too hard, or you'll blow it out." Such a level of control and respect for the fire is, arguably, something that is just not possible if the children were unable to take responsibility for managing it. The benefits of this freedom are emphasised when the young girl enthusiastically explains that, "You get to blow on the embers and you don't have to have an adult standing over you, so you get to do things with fire on your own."

PLODS

1) Design and make a homemade charcoal kiln and attempt to make our own charcoal on a fire to look at how we can keep the oxygen out of the kiln but still heat the wood.

2) Investigate what happens to wood once it burns away, encouraging a focus on warm air rising and carbon dioxide to promote an awareness of human actions on the environment.

3) Provide opportunities for decorating the candle holders using natural paints, charcoal or calligraphy to encourage creative expression.

Case Study 2 – Exploring charcoal as a material in mixtures

1. Charcoal face paint

One morning, several children gathered all the leftover bits of charcoal from the fire pit area and collected them in metal buckets. They then used a piece of wood and began smashing the big pieces of charcoal into little bits. After a while, one of the young girls put the small pieces of charcoal on a large, flat stone and then began grinding the charcoal gently into a powder. Finally, she then added this powder to an empty bucket.

When asked what she was doing, the girl replied, "We're grinding the charcoal again. It looks funny when its chunky and when you grind it with a rock, it goes all smooth."

The young girl then added water and began to stir the mixture together. Once the mixture had been made, the young girl and several other children started to put it on their arms and faces. The girl exclaimed that the charcoal, "Already has colour in it. It feels funny, cos it's kind of hard and a bit soft – we need to grind the charcoal so it's powdery, so it won't be too lumpy."

After grinding down the mixture to make it smoother, the children used the paint to draw on the green compost bin and the lid of the fire bowl in the garden. One of the older boys, then came along to see what was going on and he used the paint to create designs on his face and arms.

When he was asked about what he was doing, he replied that, "This is my tattoo made out of ash." The other children continued to create paint designs on their arms, wrote their initials on their hands, put circles on their cheeks and even lines under their eyes. When one of the staff members asked the young girl why she liked making face paint from charcoal, she explained that, "We wanted to see what it would be like to have natural face paint rather than the ones with all the chemicals and stuff." When one of the young boys had finished putting the face paint on himself, he exclaimed that, "Now we can survive in the woods." And with that, the group requested that they be allowed to go and play hide and seek in the woods.

2. Making charcoal ink

Following their interest in charcoal, the children decided to make their own charcoal ink. Two of the boys collected up charcoal into buckets and began grinding it down with sticks. When asked about what they were doing, one of them outlined the process of making the ink.

"You crush up a bunch of charcoal, add a bit of water. If it's not really a paste, add more water and if its way thin, you can add mud."

Aiden

When they had mixed the ink, the boys then used small sticks on the ground to write with. They started by writing their names and initials on different surfaces. When asked about their choice of stick, one of the boys replied that, "We didn't use green wood, 'cos we thought that would be too watery." They experimented with different sticks until they found an old stick that was used for roasting marshmallows, one of the boys explained that, "I used a sharpened stick so it's thick enough to write stuff, so you can see it. It was also quite sturdy, so it wouldn't break."

They started first by writing on rock, then wood and finally, they discovered some tree bark. One of the boys explained that, "We were trying to make it look natural, it looked cool. We just wrote on what we could find. The bark is better than the stone as it shows up better; it's easier to write on, a bit like paper."

One of the boys then decided to make a 'door hanger.' He drew a skull and cross bones on the bark and in big letters wrote, 'keep out' on the front. He then made a hole in it at the top with a nail.

Toward the end of the session, one of the younger girls carried the charcoal ink inside, whittled herself a stick using a potato peeler and sat down to draw inside our outdoor Kinder Kitchen. She explained the process of the ink saying that, "It comes from the fire, you can make ink. You get a stone to crush it. You get burnt wood. You put water in it, if you don't put water in it it won't work, you'll just get ashes on your plate. You can draw things with it. You use a whittle stick. If you don't whittle it, it will go all messy and then it won't be a pencil." Katie aged 8.

Analysis of Learning – Case Study Two

In both scenarios, the children show resourcefulness in creating their own implements for grinding down the charcoal. In particular, the young girl in the face paint scenario, shows excellent fine motor skills in delicately grinding the charcoal down onto a small flat stone. Such creativity was supported in this circumstance due to the lack of specific equipment available and the abundance of open-ended natural resources, such as rocks and sticks that the children could invent with. The exploration of the charcoal as a material, provides a range of learning benefits as the children are able to manipulate the charcoal by grinding and breaking, and are then able to change it into a mixture with the addition of water. Even from the short descriptions shown above, such as, "It looks funny when its chunky and when you grind it with a rock it goes all smooth." We can surmise that this process supports a high level of sensory input and experimentation, as well as a stimulation for the use of rich descriptive language.

In both the scenarios above, the children make mixtures out of the charcoal and show a high degree of creativity with it. For example, face paint designs, arm tattoos and the images painted onto the compost bin. The use of the charcoal ink again supports this expression, particularly when we observe the creation of the door hanger by one of the older boys. What perhaps stands out most in these scenarios is the creative expression through the use of literacy. Using the ink and the whittled sticks, the children are all motivated to write their names, initials, or important words attached to their ideas and area, and are all highly engaged in their writing. As well as evaluating the learning occurring in these moments, this also provides an excellent opportunity to develop their literacy skills both inside and outside of the classroom. In the final photo, we can see how effortlessly the use of the charcoal ink can be transferred indoors onto paper.

The two scenarios, showcase a classic example of learning through their experience, as the two boys try a range of different surfaces for writing and painting on before deciding on the most suitable surface, and the children face painting try rocks, and the compost bin before developing their face paint idea. This process is surmised when the oldest boy describes that, ". . . We just wrote on what we could find. The bark is better than the stone, as it shows up better; it's easier to write on, a bit like paper."

PLODS

1) Provide further opportunities to develop writing skills using hand-made pencils and charcoal ink on different surfaces, such as paper and linen for use inside the classroom.

2) Use charcoal as stimulation for functional, or creative writing opportunities.

3) Research body paints and find out which groups of people use them and why, to support an investigation into different groups and cultures.

4) Develop handmade pencil making using fresh wood and whittling. Support children to create their own designs.

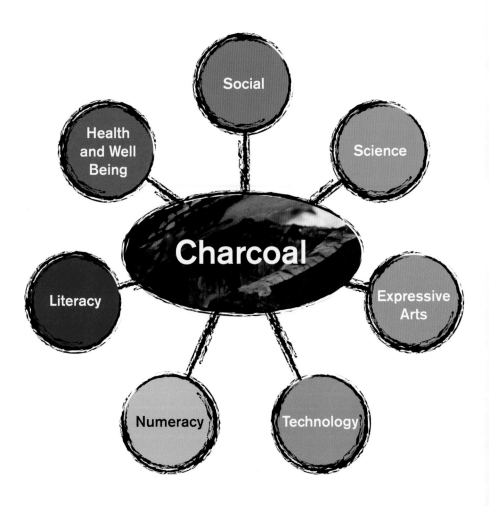

Area of enquiry

1. Conceptual knowledge of elements of a fire (Case study 1)
2. Conceptual knowledge of the effect of heat on wood (Case study 2)
3. Species of tree for charcoal use

Area of enquiry

1. Charcoal as an artistic tool (Case study 1 & 2)
2. Charcoal as provocation for role play (Case study 2)

Area of enquiry

1. Design and creation of charcoal making equipment/implements
2. Development of technology in charcoal use
3. Being resourceful with natural materials

Area of enquiry

1. Recording mathematical thinking
2. Mathematical concepts during charcoal making process

Area of enquiry

1. Charcoal as a stimulation for language and writing
2. Charcoal as a tool for writing (Case study 1 & 2)

Area of enquiry

1. Children's awareness and management of risk (Case study 1)
2. Atmospheric effect of a fire (Case study 1)
3. Active outdoor learning experiences (Case study 1 & 2)
4. Use of charcoal as a purifier

Area of enquiry

1. Historical use of charcoal
2. Natural resources in the environment (Case study 2)

Area of enquiry concept/knowledge/skill	Opportunities for experiential learning experiences
1. Conceptual knowledge of elements of a fire	
A fire needs air, heat and fuel in order to burn.	Within a small fire bowl, make a fire in the playground and discuss what the fire needs to burn. Allow children to collect small piles of firewood, either from the school grounds or bring from home.
Warm air rises. e.g. the smoke from a fire, or the steam from a kettle.	Around the fire, discuss with children what happens to the smoke once it leaves the fire. Use this as an opportunity to investigate what happens to warm air. This could link in to an investigation into the greenhouse effect or evaporation. Children as young as three will have ideas on this and it is important that these are valued and explored in depth.

Area of enquiry concept/knowledge/skill	Opportunities for experiential learning experiences
2. Conceptual knowledge of the effect of heat on wood	
When enough heat transfers to wood it burns and turns black. This is because the main component left behind is carbon, which is usually black.	Provide opportunities for children to observe the burning of a fire, or allow them to burn the end of their own sticks on the fire to observe the way the wood changes in the burning process. Conceptual knowledge can be introduced gradually according to age.
The lack of water content in charcoal makes it a brittle material which can be broken and ground easily.	Experiment widely with charcoal as a material. Once it has cooled and dried, children can break it up, grind it down, turn it into a paste to be used to make paints, inks, powders and mucky soups.
Charcoal is made when wood is heated in the absence of oxygen.	Support children to make their own charcoal kiln in a tin using small cuts of wood. If you cut small straight pieces of fresh wood, these can be used straight away as pencils.
Charcoal can be used as a resource to aid fire starting.	Using your charcoal kiln, you can heat up small pieces of cloth (preferably cotton) until it chars. As a class, this new fire starting method can be investigated during a fire session in the playground.
3. Species of tree for charcoal use	
All species of tree will make charcoal because all trees are mostly made of carbon. Trees that have a long cell length, such as willow and hazel, will work better for making pencils because they will hold together better.	Using tree identification cards (there are lots you can get from the internet), explore the school playing field or local park and try to identify the different trees in the local area. Once identified, find out which ones the children think would be good for making charcoal. They can even experiment by using different types of wood and see which ones they think work best.

Area of enquiry concept/knowledge/skill	Opportunities for experiential learning experiences
1. Children's awareness and management of risk	
Children are able to self risk assess, and the more we can trust them to make decisions and provide supportive environments for them to do so, the more they will thrive.	Children can be supported to create their own benefit risk assessment about making charcoal. This will encourage them to make decisions about how to look after themselves and others. This risk assessment can be written down by children, or recorded from their words by an adult.
2. The atmospheric effect of a fire can help support speaking and listening activities	
	Organise a reflective discussion with the children around the fire. A fire can help children to focus in on the discussion and can create a calming atmosphere. This can be a perfect opportunity to talk about feeling and emotions to do with ourselves and each other.
3. Active outdoor learning experiences	
	The charcoal making process can be facilitated into a practical outdoor learning opportunity by allowing children to take part in the collection of wood, the setting up of a safe area and the safety and management of the fire area.
	Focus can be brought to the charcoal making process to facilitate effective partnership and group working, allowing children to undertake a range of different responsibilities within a group environment.
4. Use of charcoal as a purifier	
Due to its incredibly large surface areas, infectious particles and chemicals will stick to charcoal, making it effective for air and water filtration.	Create a homemade water purification system using natural materials such as charcoal, sand, leaves and stones and attempt to purify muddy water with the children. This can be done simply in an old water bottle (see adult skills section).

Area of enquiry concept/knowledge/skill	Opportunities for experiential learning experiences
1. Charcoal as a stimulus for different types of writing	
The blackness of charcoal and its associations with death are used frequently in poems and writings across the world.	Using charcoal as stimulation, encourage children to use descriptive language or write poetry about their sensorial experience with it. The fact that children can smell, touch, break, smudge and do so many things with charcoal will mean that it is a perfect object to use as a focus for writing. It will entice visual, auditory, kinaesthetic or even olfactory learners.
	The charcoal making process and the range of other products that the children can make, provides an excellent opportunity to engage children with functional writing.
2. Charcoal as a tool for writing	
	Children can use the charcoal they have made like a pencil and use it to write with. They can experiment by writing with charcoal ink, with charcoal pencils or simply with their fingers. This writing can work well on paper in the classroom, on walls, on pavements, on trees or rocks.
3. Speaking and listening around the fire	
	The experience of sitting around a fire can create a calming atmosphere that supports children to take part in a range of speaking and listening activities.

Area of enquiry concept/knowledge/skill	Opportunities for experiential learning experiences
1. Historic use of charcoal	
Charcoal has been used for a variety of different purposes in the areas of art, horticulture and medicine, as well as a fuel.	Provide opportunities for children to research the historic uses of charcoal. If they search for this on the internet, they may discover information about who used charcoal, where it is used and what it is used for. Children can explore ways that charcoal is used at home, such as a fuel for a fire or in barbecues.
2. Natural resources in the environment	
Wood can be a sustainable energy resource if it is used sensibly and we plant and look after the trees in the environment.	Research why using wood in sensible quantities can make it a sustainable resource. The children could find out about deforestation and aforestation. The use of wood as a resource could start a tree planting project, or a conservation activity within the school, which could help raise the children's contribution to their local school environment and allow them to make a contribution to future generations.

Area of enquiry concept/knowledge/skill	Opportunities for experiential learning experiences
1. Design and creation of charcoal making equipment/utensils	
Through using a fire proof container such as tin, children can see the way that oxygen can be excluded from the heating process.	Children can make their own charcoal kilns using an empty tin. They can be involved in the decision making process about what equipment and resources to use, how many holes they should put in the tin and how big the tin should be. Children can make a variety of different implements using charcoal, such as a pencil, pen, signs, and be given the freedom to create new uses for charcoal in the school environment.
2. Development of technology in charcoal use	
The development of technology in charcoal use provides the opportunity to learn about industry, machinery and production methods.	Children can be given the opportunity to research the ways that people throughout history have used machines and resources to produce charcoal. Small rates of production using a small kiln can be compared to mass production in industry.
3. Being resourceful with natural materials	
	Charcoal is often a material that is left to rot in the fire pit. Discussing the uses of it and valuing it as a resource can provide the opportunity for utilising natural resources in the local environment. Children can learn about being resourceful with natural materials through reusing and recycling.

Area of enquiry concept/knowledge/skill	Opportunities for experiential learning experiences
1. Charcoal as an artistic tool	
Charcoal has been used by famous artists such as Picasso and Dürer and has many features that make it an excellent tool for artistic expression. The rich black colour of charcoal provides the opportunity to explore shading, tone, line and colour using different sized pieces of charcoal.	Children can be given the opportunity to use straight pieces of charcoal as crayons which they can use to draw and be creative with. Charcoal can be ground down into a powder and mixed with water to create an ink or paint. Children could use pieces of whittled wood as pencils and then be given the opportunity to create drawings. Children can experiment with different methods of creating charcoal art, such as printing, hand shading and rubbings. Children could use it to take rubbings of different surfaces outside, such as tree bark, pavements and stones to explore texture. Children can create their own charcoal paint which can be used for a range of different creative possibilities. This works well for painting indoors, but particularly well for painting in the outdoor environment as it is natural.
2. Charcoal as provocation for role play	
	Charcoal paint can be used effectively as face paint, which could be used to stimulate interest in role play and drama with children.

Numeracy

Area of enquiry concept/knowledge/skill	Opportunities for experiential learning experiences
1. Recording mathematical thinking	
	The use of charcoal pencils, ink and paint can be used as a motivating tool for recording numbers, writing sums and equations, recording measurements, or marking out shapes and areas outside in the playground.
2. Mathematical concepts during charcoal making/adaption process	
	Create designs for the charcoal kiln and encourage the children to detail numbers and measurements.
	Experiment with different sizes, lengths and thickness of fresh wood to be made into charcoal and sort these accordingly. Encourage children to measure the wood to be used for charcoal and record this in a Floorbook or diary.
	Using a stopwatch or clock, children could time and record how long the charcoal takes to make. These measurements can be recorded and taken as data and then added to any work created on the charcoal making process.
	When making charcoal ink and paint, children can create their own recipes and experiment and record the different quantities of ingredients that they used. This opportunity could focus on units of measurement.

Chapter 4. Developing Skills

1. How to make charcoal
(by Chris Warden, 16 years old)

1. Charcoal is traditionally made from lengths of Hazel or Willow.

2. You will need a tin with a close fitting lid. Make a single hole in the lid with a nail.

3. Cut pieces of green willow about 10cm in length and about 5-10mm in diameter.

4. Place into the tin, fasten the lid and use fire gloves to place the tin into the fire embers.

5. Watch as the steam plumes out of the hole. When it stops, seal the hole with some clay or mud to prevent the oxygen from entering to prevent ignition.

6. Take out the tin and leave to cool. The slow oxidation process creates the charcoal.

1. How to make an ember bowl

(by Aiden, 10 years old)

The adult prepared the pieces of wood, in this case by carving out the middle of each one with a carving knife. Children can use a hand drill with a wooden drill bit to create a depression on the top. The adult ensured the depression in the wood was deep enough so that the ember would not fall out easily (detailed on the Benefit Risk Assessment).

"This is how you make it," writes Aiden.

1. Cut down a tree and cut a bit the size you want your ember bowl.
2. You need to leave it to dry so it is not green wood, it is burnable.
3. You start up a fire until it's burning nicely.
4. Carve a little dent into the top of your ember bowl first.
5. Then put a burning ember in it. It has to fit.
6. Get a little stick over it and blow on it to keep it burning inside the bowl.
7. If it runs out, then put another ember on. If you don't give it enough oxygen, it might just burn out.
8. Let it burn down and then when your ready, you smooth it down with sandpaper.
9. It looks red, orangey and it glows.

3. How to make a water filter

(by Lara Warden, 18 years old)

Charcoal can be used to purify water. Using a natural element, such as bark to create a funnel, makes a more biodegradable version. Harvesting tree bark should be done carefully and in a way that does not harm the tree.

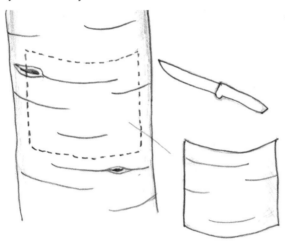

1. Cut a **shallow** rectangle of bark from a silver birch tree approximately, 30 x 20cm.

2. Pry the bark off gently.

3. Gently begin to roll the bark inward, roll the bottom end tightly, leaving a small gap approximately, 1cm across.

4. Use cordage, such as nettle stem or vine to hold the cone together.

5. Place several small stones in the bottom of the cone.

6. Layer up, alternating layers of grass, sand and charcoal.

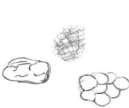

Chapter 5. Benefit Risk Assessment

Benefit Risk Assessment	Fire based activities
Assessment date: 05/2011	Date for review: 08/2011 - ongoing
Assessment undertaken by:	Staff member
Approved by:	Senior staff member
Local site Considerations/amendments:	Unstable tree branches, low level branches, overhanging area of trees, fire pit, location of fire area to building, engagement with public spaces
Benefits of activity:	• Build independence and develop trust • Opportunity for children to self risk assess • Build self confidence • Group awareness and co-operation • Aesthetics/spirituality/atmosphere of fire • Understanding the use of fire – cooking, warmth, light • Conceptual knowledge about components of fire • Experience the effect of heat on wood and the way wood changes with temperature • Exploration of charcoal making process and its various uses • Firsthand experience of carbon cycle and the use of natural resources for energy

Hazard	Level of risk	Precaution	Revised risk level
Trip hazard - material on the floor around the fire	Medium	• All are made aware of uneven ground and materials that may cause trips and slips near the outer perimeter of fire area (holes, roots, slippery mud, branches, logs, guy ropes) • Wood is collected prior to activity, sorted and stored safe distance from fire pit	Low
Inappropriate behaviour around fire	Medium	• Staff have received training in working with vulnerable groups/ are Disclosure Scotland checked • Adult ratio and positioning in area to monitor children's/ participant's behaviour near designated fire area • All are instructed to move and behave with care around fire pit	Low
Fire - burns	Medium	• Adults are trained and aware of appropriate fire building techniques and handling of fire • Gloves are available to protect hands from heat • Children do not 'feed' the fire once lit • Adults have valid first aid qualifications • Cold water available to cool burns	Low

Hazard	Level of risk	Precaution	Revised risk level
Fire - spreading	Medium	• Fire bucket with water in proximity of fire if appropriate • Fire bucket with sand in proximity of fire if appropriate • Fire blanket in proximity of fire if appropriate • Fire extinguisher in proximity of fire if appropriate • Ashes cooled with water or sand at end of session • Designated fire zone is built with own safety measures (1.5m perimeter) and is high visibility to increase risk awareness by children/participants • Choice of location for fire will be made in communication with site ranger • Fire to be kept small and controlled and staff aware of effects of weather, such as high winds	Low
Medical conditions – respiratory issues	Medium	• Allergies and medical conditions/requirements are checked prior to activity • Wood is stored to dry in order to increase effective burning (less smoke)	Low

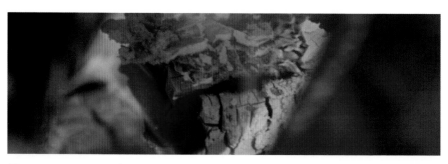

Hazard	Level of risk	Precaution	Revised risk level
Cuts or injuries - from wood handling, from hazardous plants and from tool handling	High	• Cuts are washed and treated immediately and first aid requirements dealt with appropriately • Children are monitored and supported if necessary when carrying materials. Safe lifting strategies are taught • Hazardous plants/locations must be identified in advance and contact with them prevented if appropriate • Sawing is taught as a specific skill in three stages; inside centre, outdoor area and wood. Then applied daily under adult supervision	Low
Burns sustained during post fire activities, such as charcoal handling and use of ashes	High	• Discuss temperature of fire with children, looking closely at how to tell if a fire is still hot e.g. white ash • Only allow children to access fire area when supervised by an adult/teacher • Ensure activities involving charred wood or ash from a fire are introduced at a suitable time after fire	Low
Burns sustained during activities involving use of the fire e.g. smoke sticks, ember bowls	High	• Ensure that such activities are introduced progressively and only when children are ready • Procedures for controlling embers and flames are established with children • Children are monitored and supported closely • Have low ratios to support supervision e.g. use of parent volunteers and class assistants • Ensure staff member is competent at managing a group around a fire	Medium

Summary

As humans, we have disconnected ourselves from nature and all its elements, we need to find a pathway back. This book about the element of fire, explores the place of fire as a provider. It gives us warmth, a sense of security, a source of fuel that can create and alter materials, such as dough into bread, fruit into jam, or wood into charcoal. The awareness of fire has been reduced as houses we live in are centrally heated and even cooking outside has become transformed to a gas barbecue. Children's fascination with candles on their birthday cake demonstrates the way that the movement of the flames engage children, they are aware from an early age of the hazard of heat. As adults, we assume that a visual flame is more hazardous than a hot water pipe, and yet visual cueing is a very important part of the benefit risk assessment process.

This book has been created to support adults to see the benefits of working with the natural elements as a way of teaching and learning. The inclusion of curriculum concepts and skills lead to longer term developments in attitude, that stay with the learner throughout their lives. We need to be able to identify and document learning outside, to reinforce links across three learning environments of inside, outside and beyond, if we are to support children, families and educational groups to 'be' outside in nature.

If you are enjoying this book, I would suggest you explore the other titles in the series that are, Fire, Earth, Water and Air.

With kind regards

C. Warden.

Do keep in touch through **www.claire-warden.com**
or through the publishers **www.mindstretchers.co.uk**

Mindstretchers Publications

A new series of books that provide an insight into the knowledge you need as an adult to facilitate learning occurring in outdoor environments. Includes case studies with analysis and Possible Lines of Development (P.L.O.D) with full colour photography throughout.

'The true value of this little gem...is that it respects the power of allowing children to have their own adventures, follow their own imaginations and make their discoveries'. Tim Gill

Available in 2012, a series of 4 Fascinations: Fire; Earth; Water; Air.

Price £9 (A5 paperback)

Nature Kindergartens and Forest Schools by Claire Warden - *2nd revised edition*

Claire Warden shares her extensive knowledge and expertise about her philosophy and the practicalities of creating Nature Kindergartens and Forest Schools around the globe. Includes academic research and case studies with full colour photography throughout.

Price £29 (A4 paperback)

Other Mindstretchers titles written by Claire Warden

Nurture Through Nature – Natural play for 0-3 years £25

Talking and Thinking Floorbook – Consulting with children £20

Potential of a Puddle – Vision and values for outdoor play £20

Right to Be Me – Parents and communities £20

Find out more and order online at **www.mindstretchers.co.uk**

Published by

Mindstretchers™

Email enquiries@mindstretchers.co.uk

Tel +44(0)1764 664 409 **Fax** +44(0)1764 660 728

Inspirational Learning, Inside, Outside and Beyond